MAPPING
AFRICAN-AMERICAN
HISTORY

MAPPING AFRICAN-AMERICAN HISTORY

Arwin D. Smallwood

Bradley University

Boston   Burr Ridge, IL   Dubuque, IA   Madison, WI   New York   San Francisco   St. Louis
Bangkok   Bogotá   Caracas   Kuala Lumpur   Lisbon   London   Madrid   Mexico City
Milan   Montreal   New Delhi   Santiago   Seoul   Singapore   Sydney   Taipei   Toronto

McGraw-Hill Higher Education

*A Division of The **McGraw-Hill** Companies*

ISBN: 0-07-256590-X

1 2 3 4 5 6 7 8 9 0 QPD/QPD 0 9 8 7 6 5 4 3 2

Publisher, Lyn Uhl; *sponsoring editor,* Steve Drummond; *development editor,* Kristen Mellitt; *production editor,* Jennifer Mills; *manuscript editor,* Margaret Moore; *art director,* Jeanne Schreiber; *interior and cover designer,* Cassandra Chu; *art manager,* Robin Mouat; *art editor,* Cristin Yancey; *illustrators,* Rennie Evans and Patti Isaacs; *production supervisor,* Rich DeVitto. The text was set in 12/18 Garamond Semibold by TBH Typecast, Inc. and printed on 50# Scholarly Matte by Quebecor World, Inc.

www.mhhe.com

To Justin and Raina

CONTENTS

Preface   ix

1   *Early West and North African Empires Before European Intrusion*   **1**

2   *North African Muslims (Moors) and Their Influence in Portugal, Spain, France, and the Middle East (733–1492)*   **3**

3   *Trans-Atlantic Slave Trade and the European and African Nations Enriched by the Trade (1502–1888)*   **5**

4   *English Colonial Slavery in the New England Colonies, Middle Colonies, Southern Colonies, and Caribbean (1620–1776)*   **7**

5   *Emancipation of Slaves in the North and Expansion of Slavery in the South (1777–1800)*   **9**

6   *Impact of the Three-Fifths Compromise and Northwest Ordinance on Slavery in the United States (1787)*   **11**

7   *Upper and Lower South and the Domestic Slave Trade (1808–1865)*   **13**

8   *Slave Revolts and Maroon Communities in the United States (1800–1865)*   **15**

9   *The Missouri Compromise and Its Impact on Slavery in the United States (1819–1821)*   **17**

10   *The Underground Railroad During the Civil War (1861–1865)*   **19**

11   *Major Civil War Battle Sites Involving Black Soldiers (1863–1865)*   **21**

12   *Northern States and Radical Republicans: Military Reconstruction, Establishment of the Freedmen's Bureau, and Negro State Militias (1865–1877)*   **23**

13   *Southern White Resistance to Reconstruction and the Birth of the Ku Klux Klan (1866)*   **25**

14   *First Historically Black Colleges and Universities in the South During Reconstruction (1865–1877)*   **27**

15   *Thirty Years of Lynching and the Rise of the New Ku Klux Klan in the United States (1889–1925)*   **29**

16   *Major World War I Battle Sites Involving Black Soldiers (1917–1918)*   **31**

17   *The Red Summer of 1919*   **33**

18 *Artistic and Intellectual Centers of the Harlem Renaissance (1920–1930)* **35**

19 *Rise of the Black Tenant Farmers Union in the South and Black Labor Unions in the North (1932–1945)* **37**

20 *World War II Military Training Centers for Blacks in the United States (1941–1945)* **39**

21 *Deployment of Black Troops During World War II (1941–1945)* **41**

22 *The Great Migration Continues: Blacks Moving North (1930–1980)* **43**

23 *Major Events of the Civil Rights Movement (1955–1970)* **45**

24 *End of the Great Migration: Blacks Return to the South (1980–1995)* **47**

25 *South Africa and the World in the Post–Apartheid Era* **49**

PREFACE

The importance of knowing and understanding geography and its impact on the particulars of history has been known for quite some time. Atlases and maps have been designed for or integrated into American, European, and world history for years. Until recently the same could not be said for African-American history. This workbook is designed to remedy that deficiency and assist students in learning the political and historical geography of African Americans through exercises using maps. This workbook is divided into twenty-five chapters covering the most significant events in African and African-American history. Each chapter contains one map exercise with at least four questions. These exercises ask students to identify continents, countries, states, cities, routes, rivers, lakes, and major events in African and African-American history.

Teachers and students alike will find this workbook easy to use and understand. Students will learn to read maps and identify the locations of major historical places and events as they relate to people of African descent around the world. They will also be able to note the impact of these events and places on Africans and African Americans throughout not only the United States but also the Caribbean, North and South America, Africa, Europe, and the rest of the world. Teachers and students will learn to master not only U.S. geography but world geography as well. Teachers who want to integrate African-American history into their classes and ensure that the fundamentals of African-American history—the fundamentals of any good history course—are learned will find this workbook useful and meaningful.

An answer key featuring complete versions of the maps and answers to the exercises included in the workbook is available online at www.mhhe.com/franklin. Instructors should contact their local McGraw-Hill sales representative for access instructions.

I would like to thank a number of people who assisted me in preparing this workbook. My editors, Lyn Uhl, Steve Drummond, and Kristen Mellitt deserve thanks for proposing this workbook and supporting it. I would also like to thank Jen Mills, Cassandra Chu, Cristin Yancey, Robin Mouat, Margaret Moore, and Rich DeVitto for guiding the book through the production process. Finally, I would like to thank Onno Brouwer, Associate Director, and Eric Rundell, Cartographic Student Assistant, of the Cartography Laboratory at the University of Wisconsin at Madison.

Chapter 1 | *Early West and North African Empires Before European Intrusion*

INTRODUCTION

People of African descent in the New World can, for the most part, trace their ancestry back to the myriad West African city-states of the Middle Ages. West Africans and other Africans organized political institutions according to their needs, creating, in many cases, well-developed multi-ethnic states all over the continent.

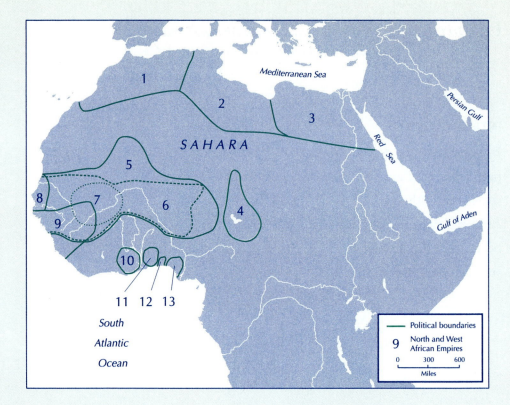

USING THE MAP

1. **Locate and identify the three greatest West African empires that rose and fell from 900 to 1800.**

2. **The Nile River, which causes the Sahara Desert to come to life along its banks, flowed through which North African empire?**

3. **The Senegal River flowed through which two coastal West African empires?**

4. **What lake was located in the kingdom of Kanem-Bornu and provided fish and freshwater?**

5. **Locate and identify the six West African empires formed as a result of the Atlantic slave trade.**

Chapter 2 | *North African Muslims (Moors) and Their Influence in Portugal, Spain, France, and the Middle East (733–1492)*

INTRODUCTION

The peoples of West and North Africa created and maintained their own unique cultures for hundreds of years before contact with Europeans, Asians, or Arabs. But clearly since 610, Islam —which spread from Mecca and Medina to Asia, Europe, and Africa—has profoundly altered the political, social, religious, and economic institutions of the continent.

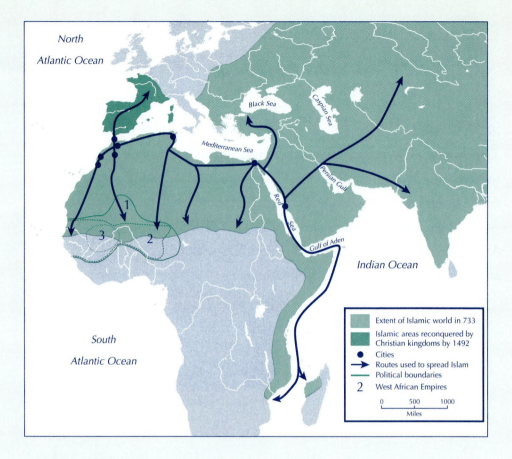

USING THE MAP

1. Identify the three great West African empires that were stimulated by trade with Islamic empires in North Africa and Southern Europe.

2. West Africans, like most Africans, maintained oral traditions and handed down supernatural and moral tales, proverbs, epic poems, satires, love songs, funeral pieces, and comic tales. After contact with Islam, many of these oral genres were recorded in Arabic and housed at West Africa's greatest university located where?

3. Identify the seven North African cities to which Islam spread.

4. Locate and identify the holiest city for Black, Arab, and White Muslims.

Chapter 3

Trans-Atlantic Slave Trade and the European and African Nations Enriched by the Trade (1502–1888)

INTRODUCTION

Slavery has been practiced all over the world for hundreds of years. Conquered peoples almost always became slaves. The Spanish brought the first African slaves to the New World in 1502. New World slavery, or the Atlantic System as it eventually was known, became the worst form of slavery in human history. First practiced by the Spanish and Portuguese in the Caribbean, North America, and South America, it was adopted by the Dutch, Swedish, French, and English who also, through war with Spain, secured colonies in the Western Hemisphere. Although Africans were also soldiers, sailors, and explorers for all of these Europeans, by the mid-1600s they had become for the most part slave labor. This made them extraordinarily valuable to the Europeans and the African kingdoms, which traded them.

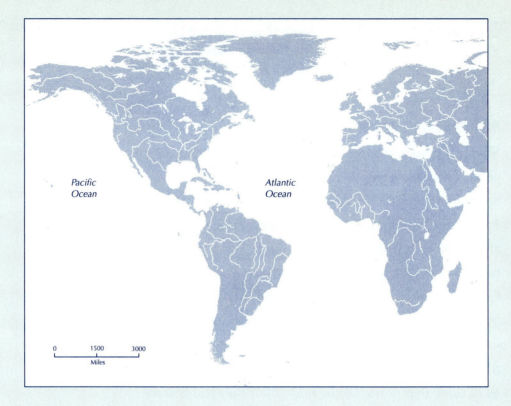

Pacific
Ocean

Atlantic
Ocean

0   1500   3000
Miles

USING THE MAP

1. **Locate and identify North America and the area of the thirteen colonies that practiced slavery during the colonial period.**

2. **Locate and identify the European nations involved in slave trading to the New World.**

3. **Locate the ocean that was crossed during the slave trade to the New World.**

4. **Locate and identify where Africans were first introduced as slaves in the New World.**

Chapter 4 | *English Colonial Slavery in the New England Colonies, Middle Colonies, Southern Colonies, and Caribbean (1620–1776)*

INTRODUCTION

Slavery was practiced everywhere in the thirteen original colonies. It was, however, practiced differently from region to region. The slaves of the New England and Middle colonies were primarily servants or dockworkers loading and unloading ships. The slaves of the Southern colonies were also servants and dockworkers, but their primary job was as plantation labor on tobacco, rice, and indigo plantations around the South.

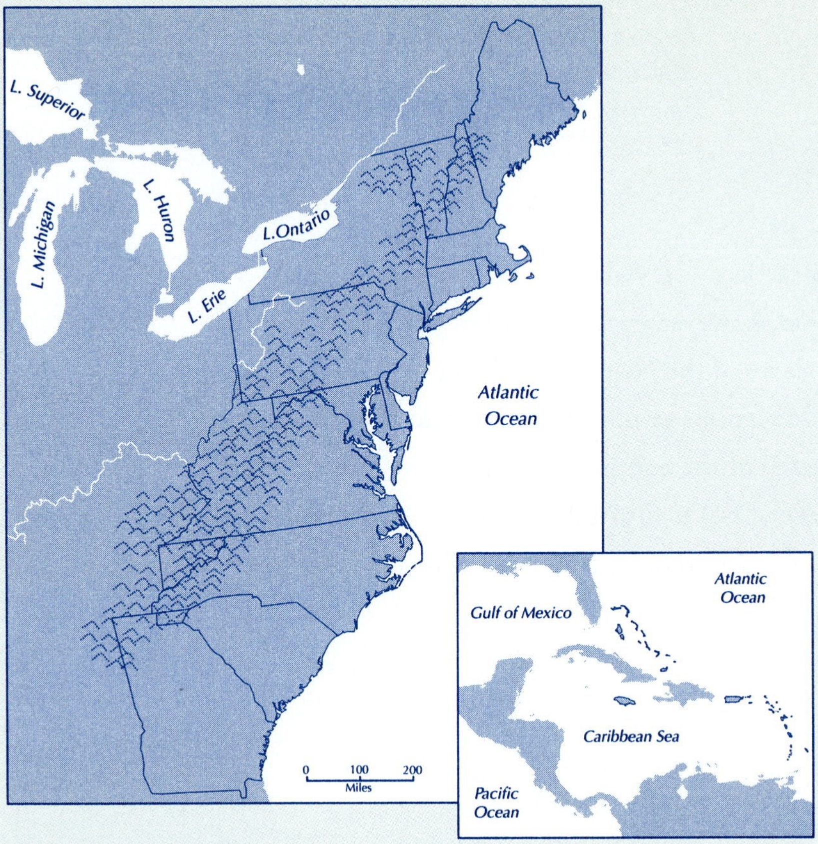
L. Superior
L. Michigan
L. Huron
L. Ontario
L. Erie
Atlantic
Ocean
0 100 200
Miles
Gulf of Mexico
Atlantic
Ocean
Caribbean Sea
Pacific
Ocean

USING THE MAP

1. **Locate and identify the Southern colonies.**

2. **Locate and identify the Middle colonies.**

3. **Locate and identify the colonies that had the least number of slaves.**

4. **Locate and identify the regions in British America where slaves were seasoned.**

Chapter 5

Emancipation of Slaves in the North and Expansion of Slavery in the South (1777–1800)

INTRODUCTION

During the American Revolution, both free and enslaved blacks fought. They fought for both sides, the British and the American. Those who supported the British were evacuated when the British withdrew from the colonies in 1783. The blacks who served with the Americans were left in a new nation split over the issue of slavery and the status of both free blacks and slaves as it pertained to their new nation.

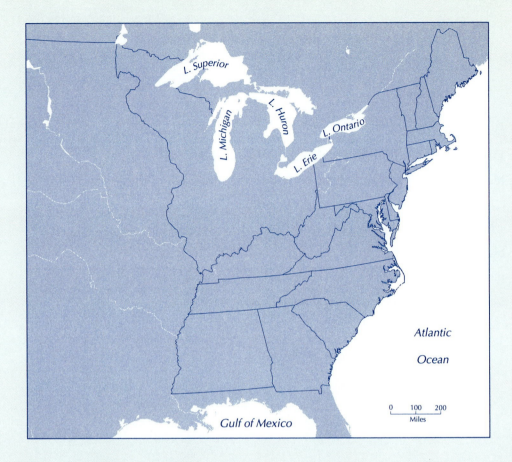

USING THE MAP

1. **Locate and identify the states that banned slavery when they drafted their state constitutions.**

2. **Locate and identify the states that refused to emancipate slaves.**

3. **Locate and identify the territory where slavery was banned in 1787.**

4. **Locate and identify the territory where slavery was allowed in 1787.**

5. **Locate and identify the states that called for gradual emancipation in their state constitutions.**

Chapter 6

Impact of the Three-Fifths Compromise and Northwest Ordinance on Slavery in the United States (1787)

INTRODUCTION

By 1800 slavery was becoming a major part of the culture of the American South and rapidly losing popularity among whites in the North. As the nation grew and expanded, it was clear that blacks and slavery would remain part of the development of the new Republic.

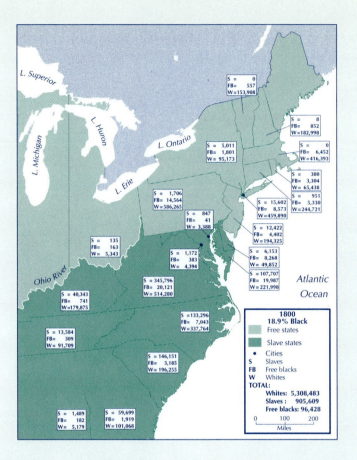

USING THE MAP

1. **Identify the state that by 1800 had a black majority.**

2. **Identify the states that had the lowest number of blacks in relation to the white population.**

3. **Identify the states where blacks made up 18.9 percent or more of the black and white population.**

4. **Locate and identify the territory north of the Ohio River which was closed to slavery.**

5. **Locate and identify the territory south of the Ohio River which was open to slavery.**

Chapter 7 | *Upper and Lower South and the Domestic Slave Trade (1808–1865)*

INTRODUCTION

As Americans fulfilled their "manifest destiny," they took their slaves with them. Slaves were and always had been everywhere in American society. In the Southwest they were pioneers, explorers, guides, skilled hunters, fishermen, and go-betweens with the Indians. They fought in America's wars of expansion and played a major role in the settlement of the southern frontier. In the South, "manifest destiny," along with conquests, aided the expansion of slavery. During this expansion, the need for slaves grew as the nation outlawed the international slave trade in 1808. As a result, the domestic slave trade was born. During this trade, black girls as young as thirteen were bred to produce slaves in the Upper South that were then sold to the Lower South where the need for slaves was the greatest.

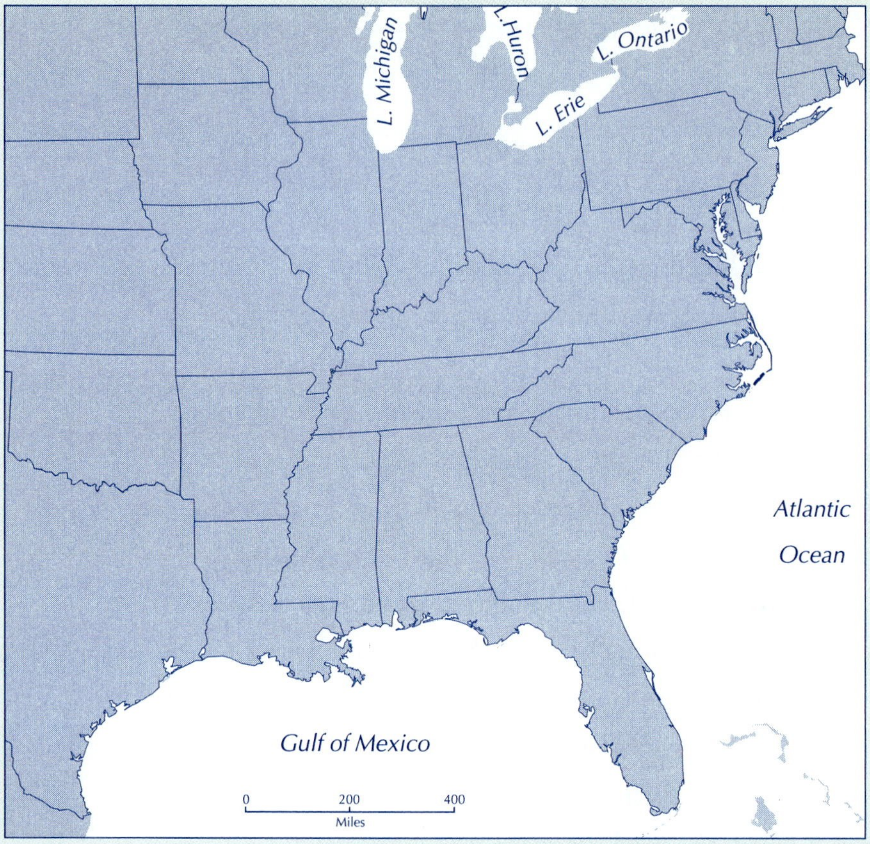
L. Michigan
L. Huron
L. Ontario
L. Erie
Atlantic
Ocean
Gulf of Mexico
0
200
400
Miles

USING THE MAP

1. **Locate and identify the slave-breeding states of the Upper South.**

2. **Locate and identify the cities involved in the domestic slave trade that were considered hubs.**

3. **Draw the routes used to trade slaves during the domestic slave trade.**

4. **Locate and identify the states of the Lower South.**

Chapter 8 | *Slave Revolts and Maroon Communities in the United States (1800–1865)*

INTRODUCTION

From 1800 to 1865, slavery was institutionalized in the South and altered the culture of all who lived there. Slaves did everything for whites in the South. They built houses, raised children, cooked meals, and labored in the fields, enriching their masters and Africanizing the entire region. In all, the "peculiar institution" lasted for more than 250 years in the South but it was not without incident. From the beginning, slaves showed their dislike of the institution by running away and joining the Indians, creating maroon communities, and revolting. Throughout colonial slavery, from Jamaica to South Carolina, numerous revolts were recorded. Although stricter slave codes were enacted to control slaves and stop revolts, from 1800 to 1865 the South would be shaken by several bloody insurrections.

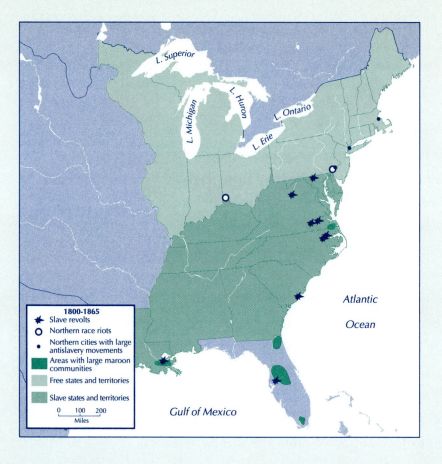

USING THE MAP

1. **Locate, name, and date the major slave revolts that occurred in the United States from 1800 to 1865.**

2. **Identify the swampy areas where maroons lived in the United States from 1800 to 1865.**

3. **Identify the Northern cities that had race riots from 1800 to 1865.**

4. **Identify the Northern states and cities that had large antislavery movements from 1800 to 1865.**

Chapter 9

The Missouri Compromise and Its Impact on Slavery in the United States (1819–1821)

INTRODUCTION

From 1787 until 1819, the nation developed half slave and half free. By 1819 the issue of where slavery and slaves should be allowed began to strain relations between the two regions. To end the tension and avert secession, a compromise was reached that became known as the Missouri Compromise. This compromise divided the nation into halves along the 36° 30' line and mandated that after Missouri no more slave states were to enter the Union above this line.

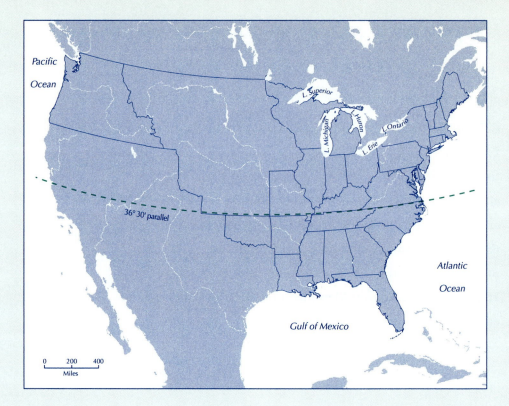

Pacific Ocean

L. Superior

L. Michigan L. Huron L. Ontario

L. Erie

36° 30' parallel

Atlantic Ocean

Gulf of Mexico

0   200   400
Miles

USING THE MAP

1. Locate and identify the slave states that were on the north side of the 36° 30' line.

2. Locate and identify the two states that came into the Union under the Missouri Compromise.

3. Which territories were considered free under the Missouri Compromise?

4. Which territories were considered slave under the Missouri Compromise?

5. Locate and identify the free states at the time the Missouri Compromise was reached.

Chapter 10

The Underground Railroad During the Civil War (1861–1865)

INTRODUCTION

By 1860 the issue of slavery had once again reached a crisis point. In question again was where slavery could be practiced. The Missouri Compromise and the Compromise of 1850 had resolved the issue, but beginning with the Dred Scott decision of 1857 and the expansion of the concept of "popular sovereignty" in 1854, the tension surrounding the issue threatened to tear the nation apart. One of the major causes of this tension was the return of runaway slaves, which Southerners demanded under the Fugitive Slave Act and antislavery activists in the North condemned. During the Civil War, more than 100,000 slaves found their way to freedom on the Underground Railroad.

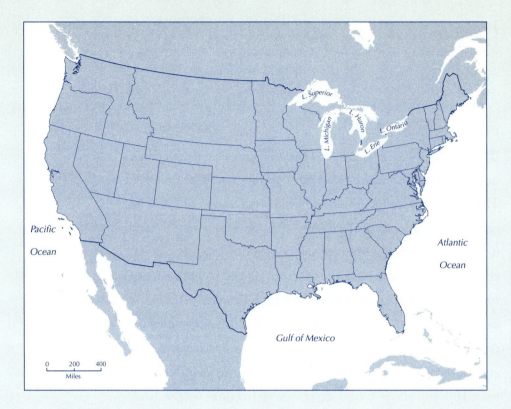

Pacific
Ocean

Atlantic
Ocean

L. Superior

L. Michigan L. Huron L. Ontario

L. Erie

Gulf of Mexico

0   200   400
Miles

USING THE MAP

1. **Locate and identify the free states and territories at the start of the Civil War.**

2. **Locate and identify the slave states and territories at the start of the Civil War.**

3. **Locate and identify the Indian reservations and communities that assisted slaves on the Underground Railroad.**

4. **Locate and identify the Southern cities that were involved in the Underground Railroad.**

5. **Draw the routes that slaves used to escape to the North during the Civil War.**

Chapter 11 | *Major Civil War Battle Sites Involving Black Soldiers (1863–1865)*

INTRODUCTION

When the Civil War broke out in 1861, it was considered by both sides to be a white man's war. From the beginning, however, abolitionist whites and blacks and runaway slaves saw it as much more. Slaves in the South ran away and joined Union forces as soldiers and laborers. Northern antislavery groups petitioned Lincoln and Congress to allow blacks to fight and abolish slavery. By the end of the war, nearly 200,000 blacks had served and 38,000 had given their lives in hundreds of battles all over the South.

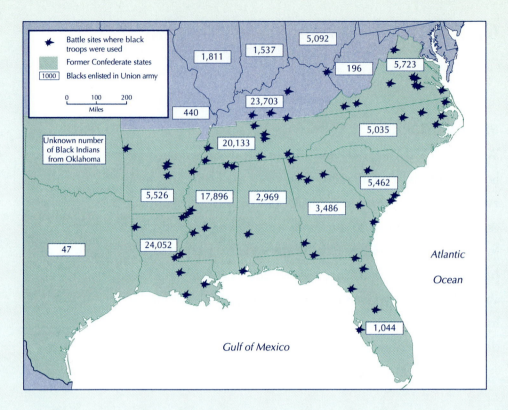

Battle sites where black troops were used

Former Confederate states

1000 Blacks enlisted in Union army

0   100   200
Miles

Unknown number of Black Indians from Oklahoma

5,092
1,811
1,537
196
5,723
23,703
440
5,035
20,133
5,526
17,896
2,969
5,462
3,486
47
24,052
1,044

Atlantic Ocean

Gulf of Mexico

USING THE MAP

1. **Identify the Southern states in the Confederacy where black Union troops were enlisted.**

2. **Identify the Northern state that enlisted the most blacks during the war.**

3. **Identify the major battle sites that involved black troops in Virginia, North Carolina, and Georgia.**

4. **Identify the Southern state that had the largest number of blacks enlisted in the Union army.**

Chapter 12

Northern States and Radical Republicans: Military Reconstruction, Establishment of the Freedmen's Bureau, and Negro State Militias (1865–1877)

INTRODUCTION

When the Civil War ended in 1865, hundreds of thousands of people, white and black, had been displaced. They were homeless, without food, shelter, or work. The war had brought ruin to the South and the people who lived there. To restore order and bring peace, the U.S. Congress divided the South into five military districts and established the Freedmen's Bureau to feed, clothe, and educate former slaves and poor whites.

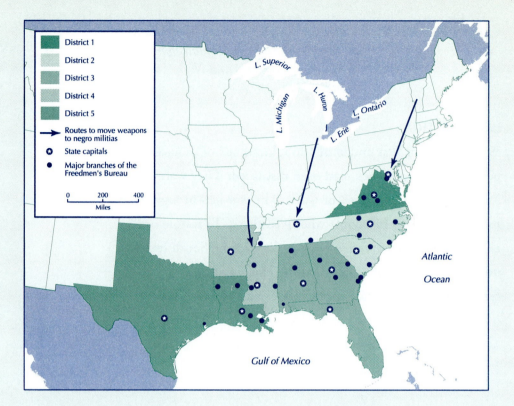

USING THE MAP

1. **Identify the location of the major branches of the Freedmen's Bureau.**

2. **Identify the Southern state capitals, which also contained branches of the Freedmen's Bureau.**

3. **Identify the Southern states in each of the five military districts during congressional Reconstruction.**

4. **Identify the states that supplied weapons to negro state militias in the South.**

Chapter 13 | *Southern White Resistance to Reconstruction and the Birth of the Ku Klux Klan (1866)*

INTRODUCTION

Although the South was defeated during the Civil War and slaves emancipated, the war never truly ended for blacks and Union supporters in the South. Former slaves and progressive whites were threatened, beaten, raped, and even killed for supporting Reconstruction and the Republican Party. These atrocities led to violent clashes between former white Confederates turned terrorist. Southern whites created a host of these organizations, but the most well known and popular was the Ku Klux Klan. As a result of the establishment of these groups, by 1877 Northerners gave up trying to reconstruct the South and allowed for the restoration of the pre–Civil War governments in the region.

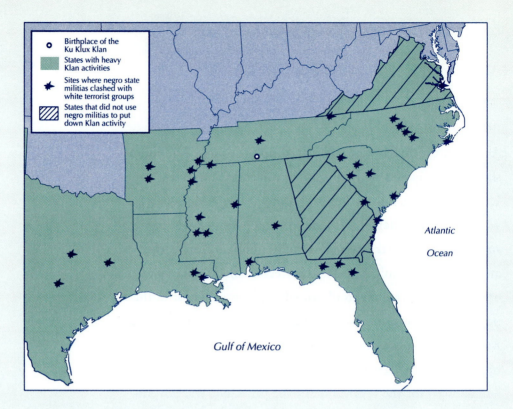

USING THE MAP

1. **Identify the city and state of the birthplace of the Ku Klux Klan.**

2. **Locate and identify the state with the most Klan activity.**

3. **Identify the states where clashes took place between negro militias and white terrorist groups.**

4. **Identify the states that did not use negro militias to combat Klan activity.**

5. **Locate and identify the city and state where the Hamburg Massacre occurred.**

Chapter 14 | *First Historically Black Colleges and Universities in the South During Reconstruction (1865–1877)*

INTRODUCTION

During Reconstruction it became clear that if former slaves were going to survive and prosper in the South, they would require job opportunities and a quality education. In response to this, many blacks immediately built churches that also served as schools and, through contracts negotiated by the Freedmen's Bureau, began to sharecrop and tenant farm. They were assisted by groups such as the U.S. government, the American Missionary Society, the Freedmen's Aid Society, and churches of various denominations, particularly Baptist. Philanthropists and black leaders helped to establish and fund nearly fifty black colleges and hundreds of churches and schools throughout the South from 1865 to 1877.

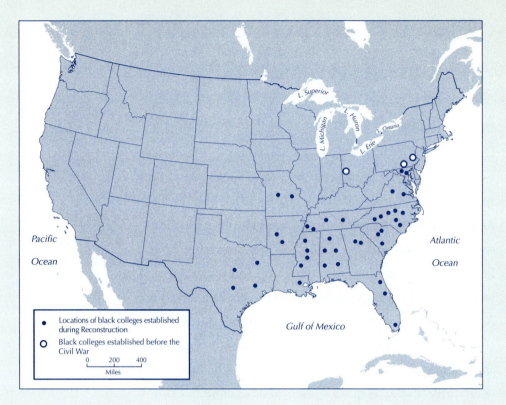

USING THE MAP

1. **Identify the Southern states that established black colleges during Reconstruction.**

2. **Identify the states and cities that established black colleges before 1865.**

3. **Locate Hampton Institute, which was one of the first black colleges established and which educated Booker T. Washington.**

4. **Which state established the most black colleges during Reconstruction?**

Chapter 15 | *Thirty Years of Lynching and the Rise of the New Ku Klux Klan in the United States (1889–1925)*

INTRODUCTION

In spite of discrimination, lack of resources, and open hostility and violence, blacks still made progress after the Civil War. They built numerous schools, churches, colleges, businesses, and banks by 1900. They were, however, still treated as second-class citizens in both the North and the South. In the South, Jim Crow was in full swing and the races were segregated at all times. During this period, blacks who spoke out or challenged racism or discrimination were dealt with violently. In what has become known as the "thirty years of lynching," thousands of blacks were beaten, raped, and killed to keep them "in their place" from 1889 to 1919. With the release of the film *The Birth of a Nation* in 1915, Klan membership and racial violence reached an all-time high in both the North and the South.

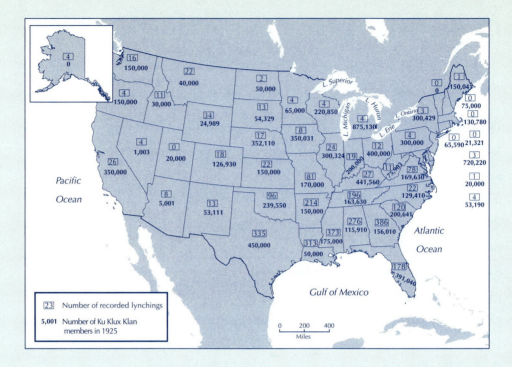

USING THE MAP

1. **Identify the states that did not have any recorded lynchings.**

2. **Identify the states that had more than 300 lynchings.**

3. **Identify the state that had the smallest Klan membership.**

4. **Identify the states that had membership in the Klan of 200,000 or more.**

Chapter 16 | *Major World War I Battle Sites Involving Black Soldiers (1917–1918)*

INTRODUCTION

When World War I broke out, blacks were among the first to volunteer for service. This service was initially rejected by the United States due to pressure from the South. When they were finally allowed to serve, many blacks received awards and honors for their service. The 369th Harlem "Hell Fighters," for example, were welcomed by the beleaguered French and by the end of the war had been awarded the Croix de Guerre (the French medal of honor) and the Legion of Honor. Their meritorious service earned them the respect of all the combatants except their white American counterparts. At home and abroad, their fellow Americans despised them and continued to mistreat them throughout the war.

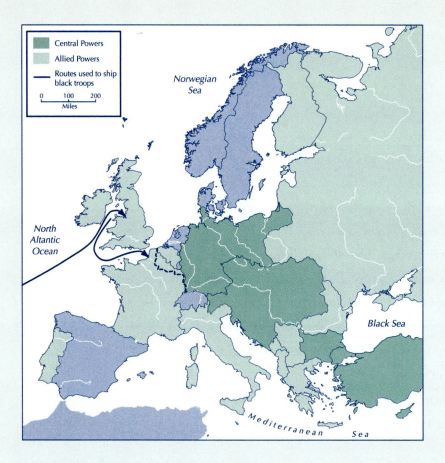

USING THE MAP

1. **Locate the trench line and the European nation where the 369th infantry fought for 191 days.**

2. **Locate the staging area and identify the nation that black troops landed on before entering France.**

3. **Identify the European nations that were members of the Central Powers.**

4. **Identify the European nations that were members of the Allied Powers.**

5. **Locate and identify the airfield where several black pilots flew during the war.**

Chapter 17 | *The Red Summer of 1919*

INTRODUCTION

When World War I ended, many blacks believed their service to the nation and the world would be recognized and appreciated. They hoped it would give them the respect and acceptance they had been striving for since emancipation. They were wrong. The American response was made very clear during the "Red Summer" of 1919. During that summer, as black troops returned from Europe, there were more than thirty violent bloody racial riots from Texas to Illinois and from Arizona to Connecticut. Soldiers in uniform were lynched, burned alive, or beaten to death. Hundreds were injured, scores killed, and millions of dollars in property destroyed.

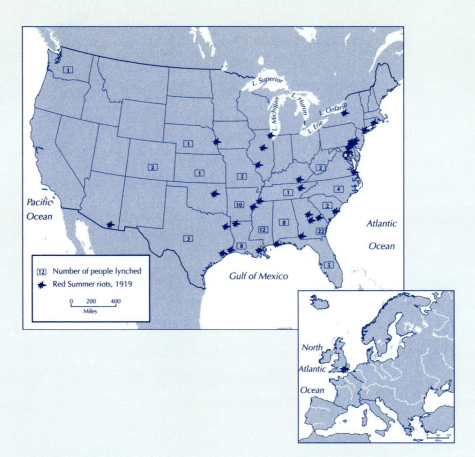

Number of people lynched
Red Summer riots, 1919

0   200   400
Miles

USING THE MAP

1. **Identify the states with both lynchings and riots.**

2. **Identify the states that had the highest number of lynchings.**

3. **Identify the states with riots but no lynchings.**

4. **Identify the European nation and locate its city that also had a race riot.**

5. **Locate and identify the European nation and its city that hosted the Pan African Conference that W. E. B. DuBois and other black leaders attended in 1919.**

Chapter 18 | *Artistic and Intellectual Centers of the Harlem Renaissance (1920–1930)*

INTRODUCTION

In spite of America's unwillingness to see African Americans as equals, much cultural and educational progress was made by blacks in the years after World War I. In Harlem and other black communities like it in the North and the South, black writers, musicians, actors, and intellectuals explored their blackness and helped to define black culture. Fueled in part by the economic prosperity brought on by the war, blacks prospered until the Great Depression of the 1930s.

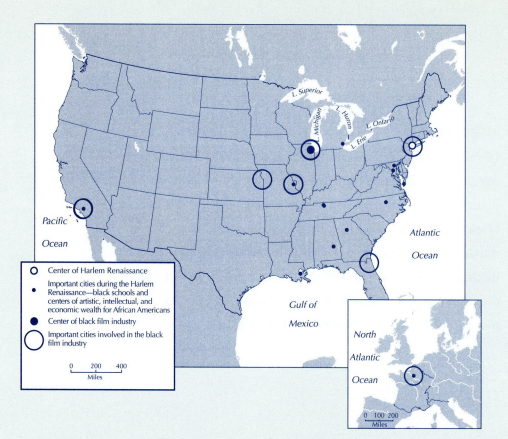

USING THE MAP

1. **Identify the city and state where the Harlem Renaissance started and was centered.**

2. **Identify the cities and states where there were black colleges and cultural centers important to the Harlem Renaissance.**

3. **Identify the center of the black film industry.**

4. **Identify the city on the West Coast which was important to the Harlem Renaissance and the black film industry.**

5. **Identify the European nation and its city that embraced the Harlem Renaissance.**

Chapter 19 | *Rise of the Black Tenant Farmers Union in the South and Black Labor Unions in the North (1932–1945)*

INTRODUCTION

From 1915 to 1929, black laborers also began to be impacted by the nation's prosperity. Low-wage labor in the North and sharecroppers and tenant farmers in the South began to organize and demand more compensation. Many of these workers attempted to establish or join existing unions to increase their wages and job security. Their attempts at organizing were often met with violence, as was the case in the Rally Massacre of tenant farmers. With the onset of the Great Depression in 1929, wage-earning blacks were compelled to continue their efforts in cities and also began to become politically active. Throughout the 1930s and 1940s, black unions in the North strengthened in membership and political influence.

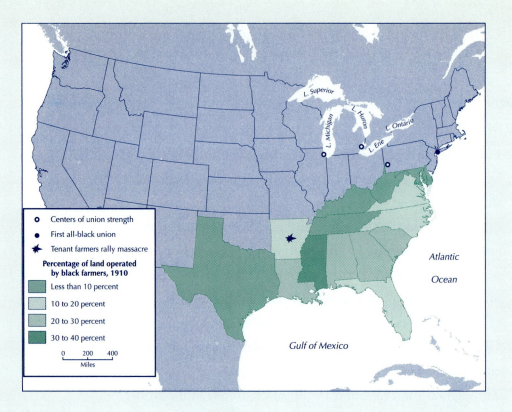

USING THE MAP

1. **Identify the cities that were centers of union strength.**

2. **Identify the city with the first all-black union, and name the union.**

3. **Identify the states that had less than 10 percent of their land farmed by black tenant farmers.**

4. **Identify the city and state where the massacre at the tenant farmers rally occurred.**

Chapter 20 | *World War II Military Training Centers for Blacks in the United States (1941–1945)*

INTRODUCTION

By the start of World War II in 1938, blacks were still struggling for civil rights. The war aided black labor by making jobs once again plentiful after 1941 with the openings left by white men who had been called up for service. Competition in a shrinking labor market assisted black labor in negotiating better labor contracts. Presidential directives from Franklin D. Roosevelt concerning government contracts also helped black labor and so did labor leaders like A. Philip Randolph. By 1943 blacks were also called into service, opening their jobs to white and black women. Those blacks who served in the armed forces were trained at a number of schools, colleges, and military bases around the country.

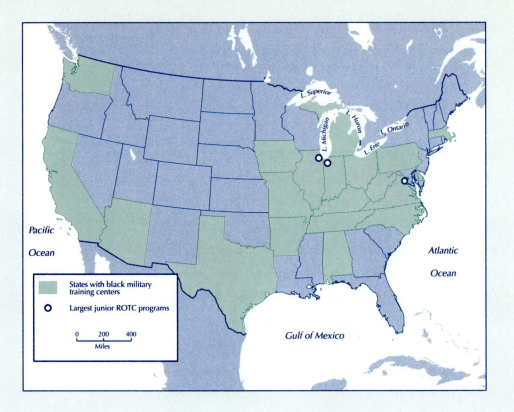

USING THE MAP

1. **Identify the states that had black military training centers during World War II.**

2. **Identify the cities with the three largest junior ROTC programs in the country.**

3. **Locate the training site for the Tuskegee Airmen.**

4. **Locate and identify the city where black enlisted women were trained during World War II.**

Chapter 21 | *Deployment of Black Troops During World War II (1941–1945)*

INTRODUCTION

During World War II blacks enlisted in the armed forces, worked in the war industries, and served as merchant marines in the face of almost certain death at sea if attacked by German submarines. They also supported the war effort by buying war bonds and doing their part at home as well as abroad. Black soldiers, sailors, airmen, and engineers fought, flew, and built bridges, roads, and camps all over Europe and the world. Black engineers braved the bitter cold of Alaska to build the Alaska Highway and the sweltering heat and humidity of the Burma jungles to build the Burma Road.

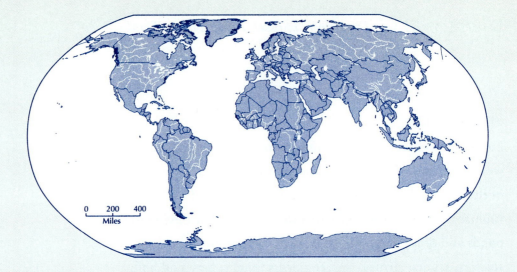

0   200   400
Miles

USING THE MAP

1. **Draw the Lend-Lease shipping routes used by black merchant marines during World War II.**

2. **Locate and identify the countries blacks traveled to or fought in during World War II.**

3. **Locate Burma, where the Burma Road was constructed with the help of black soldiers.**

4. **Locate Alaska, where the Alaska Highway was constructed with the help of black soldiers.**

Chapter 22 | *The Great Migration Continues: Blacks Moving North (1930–1980)*

INTRODUCTION

By the end of World War II and the start of the Korean War, the armed forces were integrated by President Harry S. Truman. Groups such as the National Urban League and the NAACP were helping blacks adjust to urban living in the cities they had been migrating to since 1914. These groups were also advocates for the rights of these African Americans. By 1950 the Great Migration that had been underway for more than thirty-five years was still accelerating. Millions of blacks had moved and were continuing to move to large northern and western industrial centers. This movement of people is still considered the largest in American history.

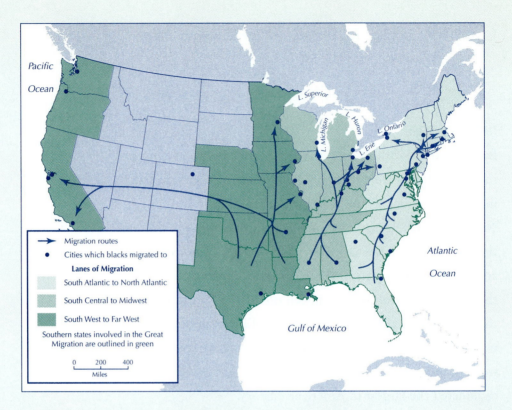

USING THE MAP

1. **Identify the states that were considered a part of the South Central region.**

2. **Identify the states that were considered a part of the South Atlantic region.**

3. **Identify the cities that blacks migrated to in the North Atlantic region.**

4. **Identify the cities that blacks migrated to in the Far West region.**

5. **Locate the city where the National Urban League was founded and headquartered.**

INTRODUCTION

From 1950 to 1980, America underwent a painful, sometimes bloody revolution. Organizations such as the NAACP, NUL, SCLC, SNCC, CORE, Black Muslims, and Black Panthers held rallies, protests, marches, sit-ins, and boycotts to force change in American society and law. By the mid-1960s, with the death of Malcolm X and later Martin Luther King Jr., young African Americans became more militant. These young people joined militant groups such as the Black Panthers and demanded immediate changes, whereas their parents and grandparents pressed for gradual change. In the late 1950s and throughout the 1960s, major events occurred that ultimately led to the demise of segregation and changed America forever.

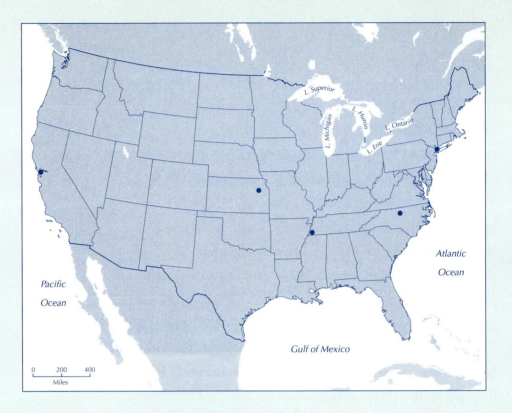

USING THE MAP

1. Locate and identify the city and state where the Black Panthers were organized.

2. Locate and identify the city and state responsible for the court case *Brown v. Board of Education of Topeka* (1954).

3. Locate and identify the city and state where Malcolm X was killed.

4. Locate and identify the city and state where Martin Luther King Jr. was killed.

5. Locate and identify the city and state where the Sit-in Movement began.

Chapter 24 | *End of the Great Migration: Blacks Return to the South (1980–1995)*

INTRODUCTION

The 1980s were very significant to the history and life of African Americans. The collapse of the infrastructure in northern and western cities, the relocation of industries to the South and abroad, and the increase in crime and hopelessness caused those blacks who could to leave and stop migrating to these cities. From 1980 to 1992, blacks also saw thirty years of hard-won gains wiped out during the presidencies of Republican presidents Ronald Reagan (1980–88) and George H. W. Bush (1988–92). Every program created during the 1960s was either challenged in an increasingly Republican court or dismantled by presidential order. By 1996 what these presidents had not accomplished, the "Republican revolution," led by Newt Gingrich in the House of Representatives and Trent Lott in the Senate, finished. Although the black middle class grew and blacks obtained recognition in sports, music, and acting, the gap between the black haves and have-nots continued to grow. It appeared the door was slammed shut on millions of poor, undereducated African Americans trapped in northern ghettos just as strides were being made to lift them out. These urban problems, along with improved conditions in the South by 1980, helped to reverse a trend that had been evident since 1914. In 1980, for the first time, more African Americans moved back to the South than moved into large northern cities.

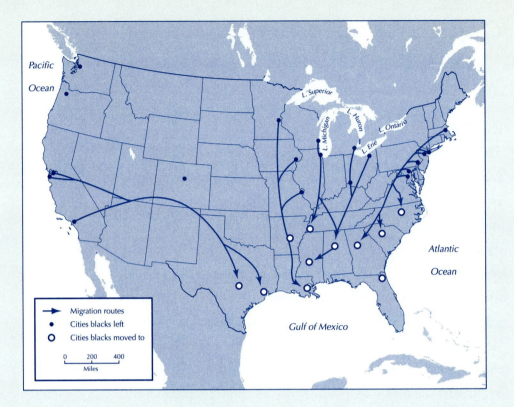

Map labels: Pacific Ocean, L. Superior, L. Michigan, L. Huron, L. Erie, L. Ontario, Atlantic Ocean, Gulf of Mexico

Legend:
→ Migration routes
● Cities blacks left
○ Cities blacks moved to

0   200   400
Miles

USING THE MAP

1. **Identify the cities and states in the North Atlantic region that blacks left for the South Atlantic region.**

2. **Identify the cities and states in the Midwest region that blacks left for the South Central region.**

3. **Identify the cities and states in the Far West region that blacks left to relocate in the Southwest region.**

4. **Identify the cities and states in the South Atlantic region that blacks migrated to from the North Atlantic region.**

Chapter 25 | *South Africa and the World in the Post–Apartheid Era*

INTRODUCTION

Although the 1980s and early 1990s were disappointing to African Americans, by 1992 with the election of Democrat Bill Clinton, blacks remained hopeful that some programs for the poor could be saved. The Clinton years, however, were filled with contradictions, and his presidency was marred by scandal which reduced its effectiveness and forced him to make concessions that tended to hurt poor African Americans more than any other group. There were, however, many positive things that occurred during the Clinton years. During the Clinton era, apartheid fell in South Africa and South Africa elected its first African president, Nelson Mandela. The United States also began to recognize the growing importance of Africa and its population of more than 817 million to future trade. By the end of the Clinton administration, Africa had become of greater interest to the United States, and President Clinton helped to ensure this by becoming the first president in U.S. history to conduct an African tour. During this tour Clinton visited many African countries, including South Africa, and pushed trade between the continent and the United States.

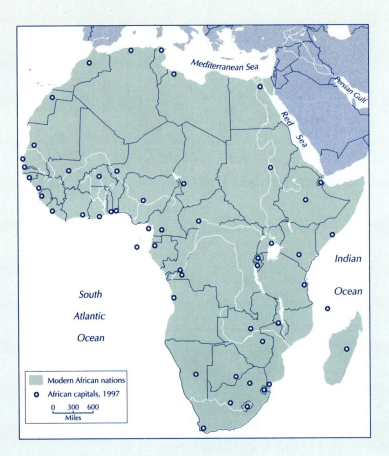

USING THE MAP

1. **Identify the African nations on this map.**

2. **Identify the capitals of the African nations on this map.**

3. **Locate and identify the African nation the brutal dictator Mobutu governed before he was exiled.**

4. **Locate and identify the African nation of which Nelson Mandela became the first African president.**

5. **Identify the African country that is an island in the Indian Ocean.**